99 tips for getting
every day in 140 cha

Time
Management
TWEETS

FOR BUSY EXECUTIVES

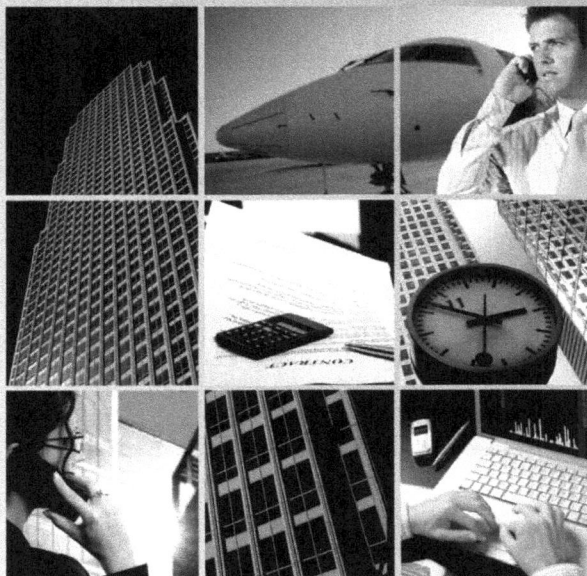

BILL BRANSON
Business Strategist & Coach

99 tips for getting the most from every day in **140** characters or less

Time
Management
TWEETS

FOR BUSY EXECUTIVES

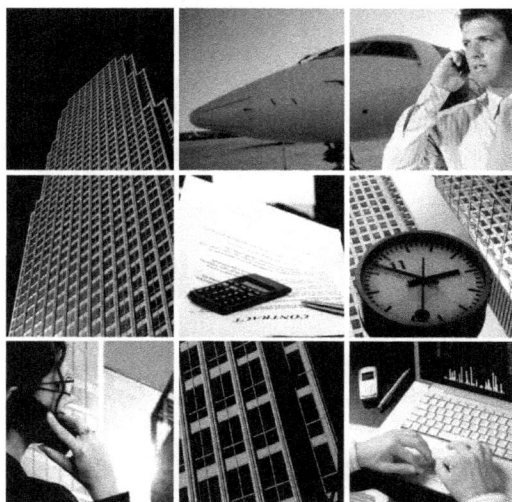

BILL BRANSON
Business Strategist & Coach

Time Management Tweets for Busy Executives
First Edition, 2012
Copyright © 2012 by Bill Branson

Order more copies from:
Strategic Business Publishers
P.O. Box 1972
Gig Harbor, WA 98335
orders@StrategicBusinessPublishers.com

Design: Bonnie Lambert, Burbank, CA
Logo and Background Designs/Branding:
    Karen Oakley, Karen Oakley Designs, Hewitt, TX
Editorial: Arlyn Lawrence, Gig Harbor, WA

Printed in the United States of America

Library of Congress Cataloging-in-Publication is available.

ISBN # 978-0-9850365-0-8

Foreword

"Time management" is simply a euphemism for focus and discipline.

Time is Mother Nature's way of making sure everything does not happen all at once. We can't control it. We can't really even manage it. However, we are responsible for what we do with our time. It is always a choice.

Some people choose to be totally fluid, flexible, and opportunistic. Others choose to be intentional and disciplined. Most successful people I know find a healthy and effective balance between being spontaneous and disciplined.

Here is what I have learned: The pathway to the next level of success is not with higher levels of activity. You are doing too much now! Nor is the road to success about going faster or working harder. You broke the sound barrier too many times this year and you already work too long and too hard. Your work style is probably not sustainable—so what are you supposed to do?

The solution can be simple! The next level of success will require the next level of focus and discipline. Commit to continuously moving to the next level of discipline in your thinking, communication, decision-making, execution, and accountability. Bill Branson presents this next level, in small increments, in this succinct but powerful book.

—Jim Horan, Author/Publisher of the best-selling *One Page Business Plan*® series

Acknowledgments

No achievement in this life is accomplished alone in a vacuum; this book is no exception. It is the culmination of a lifetime of learning, much of which comes from those who are passionate about what they do and have taken an interest in mentoring me and others like me. To them I am deeply grateful and indebted.

My life was full of mentors from a young age: neighbors, friends of the family, local business owners, managers, and teachers. All had a part in the wisdom contained in this book.

Foremost, I was blessed with a wise father, Carl Branson, who spent many hours of his time teaching and encouraging me. I'd also like to thank and acknowledge Roger C. Parker (www.publishedandprofitable) for his worksheets, templates, and candid advice, which provided a paint-by-numbers approach to organizing my ideas before I started writing. My appreciation also goes out to Kathleen Gage as a coach, trainer, and friend. Both Roger and Kathleen's coaching and formal programs on book writing and publishing, along with programs by Brian Tracy and Daniel Hall, were invaluable in teaching me how to write and publish a book.

This book is a result of a fine team of people: Bonnie Lambert for the book design, Arlyn Lawrence as the editor, Karen Oakley for logo and background designs and branding, Patsi Krakoff and Linda Dallman for their editing and writing help, Pat Schmidt and her team at DPI, Dr. Gloria Gilbère for her suggestions, encouragement, and guidance as an experienced author, Jim Horan for his mentorship, creation of the One Page Business Plan™, and for taking the time to write the foreword, and my mother-in-law, Katie Frye, for her suggestions, edits, and for loving me as one of her own.

Last but not least, I am grateful to (and for) my wife Sheree, who is not only an amazing encourager but has been the best time manager and organizer throughout our dating and marriage.

Getting the Most from This Book

Getting the most from a book is largely dependent on your personality and learning styles. Some people like to explore at a conceptual level while others are more interested in the detail. Some like to learn about the topic and think about how it affects them, while others appreciate a more prescriptive approach for putting the concepts to work immediately.

Fortunately, my styles include an appreciation for concepts, principles, and connections—the anatomy of time management—as well as a strong attention to practicality and usefulness. I like to understand and learn, but am also very anxious to put the ideas to work and get results quickly. Both of these styles contributed to this book—so no matter where you fall on the spectrum, there is something for everyone!

Here are some suggestions for ways to read *Time Management Tweets* and incorporate its principles into your day-to-day life:

1. **Read sequentially**—Start with tip number one. Read a tip at the beginning of each day for 99 days. Post the tip somewhere you will see it and try to find ways to incorporate it into the work of your day.

   Go to the TMT website and sign up for the daily tip. This will ensure you get the tip on your computer at home, laptop at work, or even your phone every day. You can choose to receive five tips a week, seven per week, or simply one tip each Monday morning. Note that frequency WILL improve results: Just reading the tips will raise your awareness and create a behavior change incrementally over time.

2. **Be focused**—This approach helps you address the areas you need to most improve by identifying your strongest and weakest areas. Our areas of greatest need generally cost us the most in the form of wasted time, frustration, and lack of results. Addressing

these areas first gives you the most leverage in the shortest period of time.

Go to the TMT website and take the assessment. You'll receive the results in your email inbox. The assessment results will help you choose which section to start with in Time Management Tweets.

3. **Get a reading buddy**—Just like having a workout buddy helps keep us on track and motivated, having a reading buddy keeps us engaged and accountable while providing some additional perspectives we may not have thought of on our own. Plan to meet regularly in person, on the phone, or over the Internet and discuss what you are reading, what jumps out at you, and how you are implementing what you are learning in your daily life.

4. **Discuss with your coach**—If you have an ongoing relationship with a coach, incorporate the material in the book in your coaching sessions. Take the assessment and share the results with your coach. Make the results a part of your program.

If you don't have a coach consider hiring one, asking your manager at work, or engaging a friend or family member to fill that role.

5. **Record your other ideas here:**

_____

_____

_____

_____

Putting the Tips to Work

You'll get the very most from this book if you'll make an effort to put the ideas from this book to work in your day-to-day activities. Here are a few ideas for doing just that:

- **Start a journal**—Purchase an inexpensive journal or use your iPad or laptop to record your thoughts about the daily tip. Read the tip; write about it.

- **Answer questions**—Use your journal to answer questions about the daily tip. Examples include:

  - Whom do you know that exemplifies the tip you just read?

  - Record your own success stories related to the tip.

  - Record your own stories about what you have learned.

  - Write down points you want to remember in your calendar, planner, or phone.

  - Ask yourself what you will do differently as a result of reading the tip.

- **Teach it**—Find someone to whom you can teach the daily tip using some of your answers to the questions above. Talk about the tip over dinner with your family. Discuss it with a coworker, spouse, or significant other.

- **Deface your book!**—Make it a practice to write down your thoughts, insights, comments, and questions. Use a highlighter pen to mark what stands out to you. Make your notes right in the book.

- **Cross-reference tips to other sources—** Make a note of other relevant sources that relate to the tip.

- **Record your own ideas here:**

_____

_____

_____

_____

_____

_____

_____

_____

Table of Contents

Introduction

Whether you're an owner of a business or an executive in a corporation, some days it's hard to get anything done. Over the course of my career, I've researched and implemented untold time management methods in my quest to become more productive. As a consultant, I've helped many clients solve their own workflow and productivity glitches.

In the process, I've discovered that some popular methods focus on strategic alignment, others on roles and relationships, and others on the nuts and bolts of execution. Whatever the emphasis however, these methods all have three principles in common:

1. **Focus** on what matters most.
2. **Engage** fully on the activity at hand.
3. **Account** to self and others on a regular basis.

So, that's exactly what we're going to learn to do, every day, in snippets of 140 characters or less.

Find creative ways to implement these tips. Post the ones that speak to you the most where you'll see them frequently. Seriously consider them. Retweet them. Talk about them to co-workers and friends—even to yourself! The more often you repeat them, the more likely they are to penetrate your daily thinking and actions.

Section 1
FOCUS

*"We are so busy
doing the urgent that we
don't have time to do
the important."*

—Confucius

Focus on
what matters most.

Consider these two questions:
What are your priorities?
What needs to be delegated?

Prioritization deals with
the "why," "what," and "when"
aspects of a task or project.

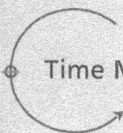

TWEET #4

4

Focus
→ Prioritization

When you are clear about
"what-needs-to-be-done," you
save time in the long run.

Capture all your
to-dos and incoming work
in one trusted place.

Create graphable objectives
that you can use to make sure
you are on track.

Write down what each
task needs in terms of desired
results. Know your goals.

Focus
→ **Prioritization**

Create a scorecard for each
key objective and
faithfully update it monthly.

Focus
→ Prioritization

Create action plans, or projects,
for the important things
you need to do to move closer
to your ultimate goals.

Create a portfolio of projects
containing no more than
5 to 7 categories.

Focus
→ Prioritization

Monitor the time investments identified in your project portfolio. Ensure they're balanced according to your established goals and priorities.

Set policies (boundaries) for
yourself. Use them to create a
time allocation plan for guiding
your time investments—
then stick to it.

"Do not squander time for
that is the stuff life is made of."
—Benjamin Franklin

14

Focus
→ Prioritization

Periodically evaluate your portfolio of projects and rebalance according to your personal time investment policies.

Examining the "why" or motivation behind your tasks is key. Is there a clear connection between your tasks and goals?

Understand the motivation
behind an objective or task—the WHY—
when determining if it is in alignment
with your key vision—the WHAT.

If your task doesn't align
with your objectives, eliminate it.
Spend time on tasks congruent
with what's needed to grow
your business.

We often leave out an
important part of task planning:
how long? Include a time
estimate with each task.

Consider setup and preparation
requirements when assessing
how long a task will take.

Include sufficient travel time
to and from appointments
when considering the total
time allotment needed.

Focus
→ Prioritization

Include wrap up and
closure time requirements
when considering how long
a task will take.

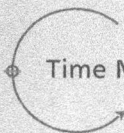

Look at the "when" requirements.
Clearly defined deadlines help you
focus towards completion.

Focus
→ Prioritization

For complex tasks it
may be necessary to have
sub-deadlines for partial
milestones.

Delegation deals with the
"who," "how," and "where" aspects
of a task or project.

Use delegation as a way to improve your communication skills and train your staff.

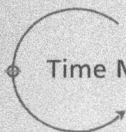

When delegating a task,
explain all the parameters of the job
both verbally and in writing
whenever possible.

Consider the level of skill and commitment of the employee when delegating tasks.

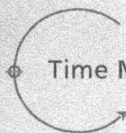

Delegating things your staff
LIKE to do will increase their
willingness to carry out
assigned tasks.

29 → Focus

Increase motivation of staff by
including them in the goal-setting
phase prior to delegating
tasks to them.

Be sure to explain the importance
of the task and how it fits into
the big picture when delegating.

Pointing out how a delegated task
directly benefits the staff member
can help increase his or her desire
and commitment to complete it.

Strategically delegate tasks that will STRETCH your staff's abilities without asking more than their CURRENT skills can accomplish.

Strategically delegate by
first working with and training
your staff members.

Include formal training as part
of your delegation strategy for
increasing your staff's abilities
and departmental capacity.

Offer to personally coach
(or assign more experienced staff
members as mentors to) staff
members when delegating
assignments.

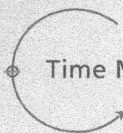

Link delegated tasks to
strategic objectives where possible
to increase motivation and
satisfaction in your staff.

Effective delegation requires awareness of one's strengths, interests, and skills, as well as those of employees, vendors, and suppliers.

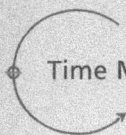

Personality assessments can enhance self-awareness and improve productivity. If you have not completed one, do so now.

Personality assessments
help you and your staff members
gain insight into what is
needed to stay in the most
productive zone.

Personality assessments
help you become aware of the
kinds of tasks and activities
that can cause stress and stifle
your productivity.

Having a good handle on your peoples' strengths helps ensure that everyone is working in their sweet spot.

ENGAGE

"You must live in the present, launch yourself on every wave, find your eternity in each moment."

—Henry David Thoreau

Engage completely in
the activity at hand.
Be fully present.

To manage your workday
successfully, try to increase the
concentration and attention
you are giving to the
task at hand.

Eliminate distractions.
Clear your calendar, shut the door,
clear the desk, and forward
the phone.

Concentrate on one thing at a time.
While you may have a high tolerance
for multitasking, your mind can
actually only focus on one
thing at a time.

Break your work into manageable chunks that can be completed in one sitting.

Get more done and gain a
strong feeling of accomplishment at
the end of the day by chunking
your work into completion blocks.

Determine your concentration
threshold. Do you work best in
increments of 10, 20, 30, or
60 minutes?

Ask yourself,
"What can I complete?"

Transform your mindset
from finishing a task (simply
removing it from your to-do list)
to completing a task (seeing it as
part of the whole, a step
in the process).

Another way to attack a complex project is to ask, "What is the next action step?" Then do it!

How you specifically accomplish tasks depends on your personality. Find methods that work best for you and stick with them.

Expand your memory;
increase your productivity and
processing power by leveraging
technology to assist you.

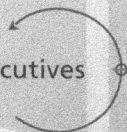

Turn off disruptive technology
during work sessions.

To the largest extent possible,
automate repetitive tasks.

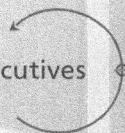

Group like tasks together:
phone calls, errands, computer
work, etc.

Speed up repetitive tasks
and reduce errors by creating
and using checklists.

TWEET # **58** → Engage

Create a filing system
that works for you. File items
immediately when you are
not using them.

Review your calendar at
least at the beginning and
ending of each day.

At the close of
each day make your plan
for the next day.

Start your day
by reviewing your
daily plan.

Record future tasks
and recurring to-dos on
your calendar.

Don't reinvent the wheel—
seek out and use best practices
whenever possible.

TWEET # **64** → Engage

Before closing a task on
your computer, save the context
of your work before moving on
to the next task so you'll know
where to pick up again.

Make it easy to find pertinent materials by creating a useful note to refresh your memory and posting it where you'll see it.

66 → Engage

Purchase a countdown timer
and divide your work into 30-minute
work segments (or other increments
as mentioned previously), using
the timer to keep you
on track.

Be sure to take a break
between intense working sessions.

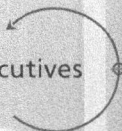

68

Engage
→ Sharpen the saw

While at work, alternate between intense mental tasks & physical work, between alone time & time with individuals & groups.

Engage
→ Sharpen the saw

Plan on taking the
long way home tonight
to break up the monotony
of your daily routine.

Take a walk during your lunch hour, or try yoga, breathing exercises,or puzzles—different things can be relaxing for different people.

Be sure to program in
time for personal recreation.

Volunteer to help others, especially those less fortunate than you. Work at a school, visit a rest home, serve at your local soup kitchen.

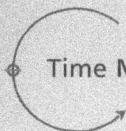

Take time to work in
your garage, kitchen, or yard.
Make time for your hobby,
whatever it is.

Engage
→ Sharpen the saw

Spend time with family
and friends—remember no one
on their deathbed ever wished
they had spent more time
at the office.

If your job has a high RELATIONAL
quotient, take time to be ALONE
away from the constant press
of meetings and people.

TWEET #

76

Engage
→ Sharpen the saw

Take your inner child out to lunch—do something today that brings out your childlike qualities—play with children or pets.

Be sure to reward yourself
for good behavior by taking
a mini vacation.

78

Engage
→ Sharpen the saw

Make time in your
schedule to exercise regularly.
Consider listening to books and
classes while you work out.

Make a list of things
you loved doing in the past but
haven't done for a long time.
Put one of these items in your
schedule each month.

Engage
→ Sharpen the saw

Pick some chores that you won't delegate. Some of my best ideas came when I was doing mundane tasks such as mowing the lawn.

Identify your common
interruptions and create a strategy
for mitigating them.

Take time each month to
stay current professionally; attend
a conference or seminar, read
an industry journal.

Be sure you and your staff
do all necessary pre-work before
key meetings.

When sending invitations for
meetings, only invite those whose
presence will be appropriate
and relevant to the task
at hand.

Assign action items as
they occur in meetings and
review them at the end.

Record and publish meeting minutes within 24 hours after key meetings.

ACCOUNT

"When performance is measured, performance improves. When performance is measured and reported back, the rate of improvement accelerates."

—Thomas S. Monson

Account to self and others on a regular basis.

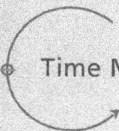

Most successful people
make it a regular practice to
set tangible objectives and
hold themselves accountable.

Choose an accountability partner,
someone with whom you can share
your goals and who will
hold you accountable.

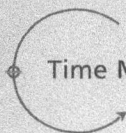

Conduct a business review
meeting each month with your
accountability partner(s).

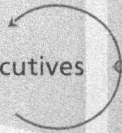

→ Account

In your monthly review meeting, review your "scorecards"— simple graphs of the 5 to 9 key objectives you designed in your business plan.

Monthly, create and review progress reports—brief summaries of key projects in light of milestones and items needing management attention.

93

→ Account

Knowing you have to
report each week or month
keeps the important items
at the top of your mind.

Monitor your progress with
the help of an accountability
partner on a regular basis.

Consider hiring a business coach as your personal trainer for getting your career or business into shape.

Keep an activity log of all
your doings for two weeks.

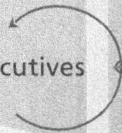

Review your activity log
and estimate the actual cost
of your activities.

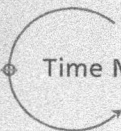

Estimate the
return value you get
from each activity.

Periodically analyze your
activities against your
long-term goals.

Resources

Want more? Here are some additional resources to help YOU get the MOST from every day:

TimeManagementTweets.com
Main website for busy executives, mentors, and educators

Time Management Tweets Email Service
Sign up for the daily / weekly email

Time Management Tweets FREE Membership
Contains periodic articles, additional tips, and tools

Time Management Tweets 100-Day Membership
Informative blog posts on each tip, monthly teleseminar, and additional bonuses

TimeManagementTweets.com/coaching
Get personal, expert coaching

Personality Assessments
StrategicBusinessArchitects.com/Personality
Take the guesswork out of your personal
productivity, satisfaction, and growth.
Learn how to optimize your life based on how
you are wired.

Business Planning
StrategicBusinessArchitects.com/BizPlanning
Extend your time management discipline into
your business. Quickly create a business plan
that fits on one page in 29 sentences or less.

About the Author

As a business strategist and coach, Bill Branson teaches business owners and executives how to build cohesive leadership teams, clarify their organizational vision, and translate their vision into a simple, actionable plan.

Drawing on his recognized leadership and management experience and his extensive experience with information technology, Bill provides consulting and coaching services to clients across the globe. His expertise also includes enterprise architecture, IT strategy, business analysis, and business process management.

Bill is also founder of Strategic Business Architects, through which he teaches business professionals how to make the most of themselves, their organizations, and their relationships.

Formerly with Russell Investment Group, Bill was responsible for creating and directing the organization's first IT Architecture Department, then the Strategic Business Architecture team within their Investment Management and Research Department.

Bill Branson's wide-ranging work history in both vendor and end user companies spans 30 years and includes IT architecture and strategy, technical marketing and support, systems and application development, and network engineering. A former instructor at the University of Washington in the areas of networking and computers, Bill continues to be a frequently sought-out speaker for industry seminars, conferences, and consulting.

TimeManagementTweets.com
www.linkedin.com/in/billbranson
StrategicBusinessArchitects.com

Time Management TWEETS for Busy Executives 99 Tips for Getting the Most from Every Day in 140 Characters or Less

by Bill Branson

Increase your happiness, compensation, and contributions to your company, career, and people ... *in 140 characters or less.*

What do "tweeting" and the busy executive have in common? Both need the impact c succinct, to the point, quick focus to be successful. Whether you "tweet" or not the concise 140-characters-or-less expression of thoughts can translate intc action that will optimize your operational excellence, efficiency, and innovation.

✔ Includes a BONUS MEMBERSHIP blog and network opportunities

✔ DAILY TWEETS via e-mail available

➤ **LEARN to manage your time,** making more of what you have

➤ **STREAMLINE the processes** you use every day

➤ **GET MORE** than simply results

➤ **PRESERVE and ENHANCE relationships** through increased responsiveness, collaboration, and recognition

➤ **GET THE MOST from your technology**

BILL BRANSON is a business strategist and coach who consults with busy executives, helping them set and accomplish their goals and get the most out of every workday